THE
DIRECT METHOD IN
GERMAN POETRY

T0346170

THE DIRECT METHOD

IN

GERMAN POETRY

*An Inaugural Lecture delivered on
January 25th 1946*

BY

E. M. BUTLER

*Schröder Professor of German in
the University of Cambridge*

CAMBRIDGE

At the University Press

1946

CAMBRIDGE
UNIVERSITY PRESS

University Printing House, Cambridge CB2 8BS, United Kingdom

Published in the United States of America by Cambridge University Press, New York

Cambridge University Press is part of the University of Cambridge.

It furthers the University's mission by disseminating knowledge in the pursuit of education, learning and research at the highest international levels of excellence.

www.cambridge.org
Information on this title: www.cambridge.org/9781107634213

© Cambridge University Press 1946

First published 1946
Re-issued 2014

A catalogue record for this publication is available from the British Library

ISBN 978-1-107-63421-3 Paperback

THE DIRECT METHOD
IN
GERMAN POETRY

NOTHING surely so much favours the retrospective mood as the emergence, however slow and precarious it may be, from the grim nightmare of a total war. Looking backwards to the past, I cannot but remember, with an affection which has certainly not decreased, the first holder of the German chair in this University—Professor Karl Breul, who inaugurated the present flourishing German School, and did so much to make German studies popular in England. With his name, those of his friends Schröder, Beit, Tiarks and Frieda Mond, munificent benefactors to the University, are now indissolubly connected. And as my mind travels back on this occasion I seem to hear again his charming and eager voice, enthusiastically expounding the beauties of German Literature, from *Muspilli* down to *Faust*. How little any of us thought then that the zeal for all things German he was instilling into us would be put to the proof not once but twice in so searching a manner. And those subsequent generations of students who were privileged to profit by the profound and profoundly humane scholarship of Professor Williams, and to whom the years 1914–1918 were ceasing to be a hideous reality, will rarely, if ever, have let their minds stray from the courtly epic or the *Minnesang* to the sinking of the *Lusitania* or the use of poison gas.

Yet, wise after the event, we cannot approach German poetry quite so open-heartedly now. We are almost forced to scrutinise it in order to discover those hidden and often unconscious layers of the minds that created it, and thus to detect the kind of relationship, whether of continuity or the reverse, which exists between the masterpieces of German Literature and Nazi ideology. The initial difficulty of such an undertaking lies in the fact that poetry is a very baffling language, which is not universally and perhaps never completely understood. The countless definitions it has undergone, none of which rings quite true, bear witness to that. Naturally enough, since the native element of art is mystery, inducing the attendant emotion of wonder, as we contemplate the fundamental mystery of life in the magic mirror of art.

The attempt to explain this riddle rationally is the task of philosophy, whereas great artists reflect it in innumerable ways according to the rules of their craft which allow of multitudinous manipulations. Underlying them all, however, are two different methods of approach to the aesthetic problem. Mystery and wonder can be evoked by creating with sounds or words, with marble or with colours on canvas what nature or life creates by other means; or by taking mystery itself as the object of art. The first method, which works by suggestion, implicitly, I call the indirect method, and its most outstanding characteristic is ambiguity; the second which is explicit, I label direct, and obscurity is its leading feature.

Music by nature is inherently direct. It must be forcibly wedded to words or descend to descriptive and onomatopoeic tricks to remind us of life and nature at all. It by-passes such manifestations, as a rule, bearing a direct communication from other spheres. Its technique certainly addresses itself to the intellect; but its seemingly cosmic significance can only be darkly felt, and can be as variously interpreted as the emotions which it arouses are indefinable and vague. It creates something

                              built
        Of music, therefore never built at all,
        And, therefore, built for ever.

How much less mysterious and how much more ambiguous is architecture. Its apparent aim is achieved by a temple, a palace, a court of justice standing for piety, kingship, order and law in their social aspect; its actual aesthetic effect involves one of the greater mysteries: the interplay of spirit and matter in its most striking form. Sculpture has more elbow-room. When merely representing human or natural objects in their victorious three-dimensional reality, it is nevertheless indirectly suggestive of the moulding of reality by the conquering power of ideas; and it can approximate to a direct effect by the use of symbolism and allegory. Like music (although for the opposite reason) it then borrows from language by giving a name to the statue or group, or hieroglyphic symbols. It can, however, also produce a startlingly direct effect. Epstein certainly does this; Siva dancing the *tandava* represents rather than suggests the mystery of creative and destructive life co-existing in the same cosmic spirit, and the Sphinx is a riddle in stone. Painting for its part often represents direct visions of the mystery of the world, as in Raphael's *Transfiguration*, but is perhaps even more skilful at alluding to its presence behind the visual aspects of life.

Poetry (in the wide sense) has the great advantage of natural flexibility. It can use either method as the spirit dictates, sliding from one to the other and back again in the course of a single poem. Indeed, few of the longer works of art keep ex-

8

clusively to either mode, and the most effective are generally composed of a skilful intermingling of both. Thus, in Greek tragedy, ambiguity haunts the dialogue, and mystery the choric odes. But strongly creative poets like Homer favour the indirect method. In the *Iliad* he seems to be aiming at a faithful and detailed presentation of an episode in the Trojan War, and to be entirely absorbed in that. One could argue, on the other hand, that his pantheon is a clear example of the direct method; and one certainly would if one lived in the seventeenth century, so hot on the scent of *le merveilleux*. There is very little mystery about his gods and goddesses, however, who actually contribute far less than the human heroes to the total impression of the inscrutable ways of life which the poem produces. Dante and Milton, although poles apart in other ways, aimed at representing cosmic mysteries as directly as possible. The more closely they approximate to that aim, the obscurer they become, notably Dante in the *Paradiso*. When they have recourse to the indirect method, the fates and fortunes of their human or superhuman heroes obscure the issue to an extent which made Satan the real hero of *Paradise Lost*, a highly ambiguous situation. The obscurity of Blake's prophetic books, even when the esoteric symbolism is grasped, has become proverbial; and although Bunyan is crystal clear, his use of allegory (the result of crossing the direct with the indirect species) satisfies the demands of neither, despite the beauty of the biblical prose and the strength of the writer's emotions. Cervantes' weapon of irony is a bridge which others have thrown across the narrow but bottomless gulf separating the two methods; and Calderon, in *La vida es sueño*, is perhaps the greatest of all those makers of dreams who have turned the bridge into a rainbow.

Shakespeare's power is very evident in his equal mastery of both methods and the manner of their intermingling. No longer willing to relegate mystery to the then archaic chorus, he caused it to intervene directly whenever occasion served: in the fantasies of Richard II, the self-communings of Hamlet, the ravings of Lear, the glosses of the Fool, the facetia of Falstaff; not to mention its incarnation in witches, spirits and ghosts and its eruption in *The Tempest*.

Masterpieces of the rival method, deceptively clear and reasonable, are among the glories of French Literature, which answered the *Divina Commedia* with a *Comédie Humaine*, and produced in Molière and Lafontaine two of the subtlest poets in Europe. But 'la fille de Minos et de Pasiphaé' is haunted by a mystery which also impregnates Baudelaire's *Fleurs du Mal* and Valéry's *Jeune Parque*, as well as Proust's conception of time. For the direct method has been gaining ground rather rapidly in Europe during the twentieth century. One can hardly imagine, for example, any present-day writer of Jane Austen's calibre (and inevitably one thinks of Virginia Woolf) who would be content to use the indirect method so rigorously and exclusively, almost as if she were unaware of the mysteriousness of life. As indeed she may have been. It is by no means easy to determine whether writers of this type have a conscious sense of mystery or not. Ibsen's realistic plays, for instance, are so misleading in their ambiguity, that an acute critic like Bernard Shaw believed them to be mere attacks upon hypocrisy, whilst less intelligent critics have misunderstood them more grossly, interpreting *Ghosts* as a sermon on eugenics, which was the gospel according to the naturalists. And yet even in these stark revelations of life, the ghost of Beate drifting (disguised as the exposition) through *Rosmersholm* is only one example of the many, sometimes incongruous, irruptions of the direct method into the plays of the middle period. Ibsen had tried to keep it at bay since the days of *Peer Gynt*, but it came into its own finally in *When We Dead Awaken*. Dostoyevski halts most instructively between the two methods, favouring the direct on all the more significant and crucial occasions. In fact he can hardly be called ambiguous at all, since one is never in doubt that he is endeavouring to convey the un-utterable and unfathomable element in life.

The sense of mystery and the feeling of wonder, vividly experienced and aroused by poets, can be communicated in one or other of these two ways, whether in epic, drama, lyric or satire, and whether in verse or prose. But lyrical poetry, cousin-german to music, is most clearly in tune with the infinite which it conveys by the magic of rhythm and words. These can and indeed very often do launch us into 'that immortal sea which brought us hither' quite independently of the ostensible or indirect subject of the poem. The explicit submerging of the latter into its native element was the conscious aesthetic aim of those poets who, in the nineteenth century and later, drew their inspiration from folk-songs. There is a world of difference between the treatment of the Olaf legend in the old ballad and in Keats's *La belle dame sans merci*. Both deal with the same mysterious situation. The ballad does not describe this aspect of it. It recounts the events in the order of their occurrence, and reproduces the dialogue between the knight and the elf-queen without com-ment. But the drumming rhythm, beaten out by avid feet, fills the air with a weird menace, later de-liberately precipitated into unforgettable words of wizardry by Keats. In the same way Heine drew from the lilting rhythm of an artless lullaby the

tragic vision of a doomed king rocking the cradle
of his future executioner.

Lyrical poetry, therefore, can range from plain
statements of such agreeable facts as

It was a lover and his lass,

through more haunting assertions, such as

Es war ein König in Thule,
Gar treu bis an das Grab,

to such bewildering communications as

Que si ta bouche fait un rêve,
Cette soif qui songe à la sève,
Ce délice à demi futur,
C'est l'éternité fondante, Ève!

For language can do many different things in many
different ways. It can assure us in the sweetly
reasonable voice of a woman, with only the slightest
stress, that

The quality of mercy is not strained;

or it can command as with the tongue of a mighty
spirit:

Lift up, ye princes, your gates, and be ye lift up, ye
everlasting doors, and the king of glory shall come in . . .

or it can dictate apocalyptic wisdom through the
mouth of a sage:

Behold! the rituals of the old time are black. Let the

evil ones be cast away; let the good ones be purged by the prophet! Then shall this Knowledge go aright. I am the Flame that burns in every heart of man, and in the core of every star. I am Life, and the giver of Life, yet therefore is the knowledge of me the knowledge of death. I am the Magician and the Exorcist.

All poets are magicians; direct poets are exorcists too.

The weakness of direct poetry lies in the fact that it often defeats its own ends, and is valued exclusively for its apparent purpose, for its content and not for its deeper significance. But used as the greatest have used it, its fundamental meaning will tell. Even those among Homer's listeners who were wholly intent on the battles, cannot have undergone that particular experience and emerged from it with their vision of life unchanged. And those groundlings who flocked to witness the horrible murder of Desdemona did not do so unscathed. The strength of this method is its widespread human appeal.

The weakness of the direct method is shown in the fact that it is liable to challenge the intellect rather than the emotions, and either prove too interesting to be enjoyed as art, or too difficult to be enjoyed at all. But used as the greatest have used it, the direct communication of mystery is perhaps the most notable triumph of poetry. From the obscurity of Aeschylus's choruses, stupendous visions arise. The strength of this method is felt in the intensity of its appeal.

It is, I think, the progressive growth in intensity which characterises German Literature since the days of Goethe. Certainly a prolonged preoccupation with modern German poetry is an exciting and exacting experience, exposed as one is to the unremitting pressure upon the mind of the great dynasty of questions (as Rilke called them) which never have been and never can be answered. And looking back beyond the eighteenth century to what went before, it also seems as if something in the nature of the minds responsible tends naturally to obscurity and mystery rather than to plastic clarity. This is, of course, no hard and fast rule; and even in the nineteenth and twentieth centuries the quantitative bulk of indirect literature probably outweighs the direct. Qualitatively, however, the situation is reversed; and after all this is only what one would expect from a race so musically gifted, so mystically inclined and so philosophically minded as the Germans. The late Professor Robertson of London University said of the content of German Literature much the same thing as I am saying for its method, when he maintained that it deals more persistently and more constantly with the individual human soul than with the external world. To which

I would add the rider, and also more successfully on the whole.

Yet the *Nibelungenlied* in the thirteenth, Hans Sachs in the sixteenth, *Simplicissimus* in the seventeenth and Lessing in the eighteenth centuries are outstanding examples of poems and persons dealing only indirectly (when they dealt at all) with eternal problems and verities. Some comments, however, suggest themselves in this connection. The medievalists are inclined to agree that Wolfram von Eschenbach's *Parzival* represents the high-water mark of European poetry in the Middle Ages, a claim never put forward, so far as I am aware, for the *Nibelungenlied*. A remarkable change had, however, come over the spirit of German poetry in the fifteenth and sixteenth centuries; and Hans Sachs and his school demonstrate one of the most sustained and determined efforts of the German genius to express itself by means of the indirect method in literature. The result is strikingly realistic, commonsensical, shrewd, humorous, lively and entertaining. But honesty compels one to admit that the achievement as a whole represents poetry in the making rather than poetry itself. One glance back to Chaucer annihilates Hans Sachs. And this was one of the reasons why the tradition collapsed like a pricked balloon in the seventeenth century. It was not nearly strong enough to resist the inrush of foreign fashions in the wake of the Thirty Years' War. Nor can one ignore the fact that Luther and not Hans Sachs was the giant of the age, and the translation of the Bible the great poetical exploit of the times. So that one need hardly mention the religious hymns and the bubbling up of the *Volkslied* to convince oneself where the real strength of German poetry lay.

Grimmelshausen's *Simplicissimus*, by common consent the one indubitable and imperishable work of genius the seventeenth century had to show in Germany, is also one of the greatest triumphs of that literature in indirect, ambiguous art. The pilgrimage of the hero's soul is represented (and how graphically and vividly) by means of the external events which befell him, or of the adventures he undertook. And yet even here the manner mysterious intrudes at intervals throughout; and the author plunged headlong into it, when his hero dived down into the depths of the Mummelsee and took his final farewell of the world on his haunted desert island, as different from Robinson Crusoe as one castaway could well be from another.

Lessing, witty and doughty rationalist that he was, was immune from such temptations, although one rather holds one's breath as one watches him gravitating insensibly towards a major mystery in *Nathan der Weise*; being Lessing, however, he

17

avoided direct expression of it when it came to the point by enlisting the aid of that ambiguous veteran, the fable of the three rings. But half-measures and compromise, so much beloved over here, do not appeal as a rule to German minds; they much prefer extremes. And in the eighteenth century a bid was made for favour by the direct method on the one hand, and the indirect on the other, in their purest forms. It was almost as if Germany were being asked to choose between them, and to swear allegiance either to Klopstock's *Messias* or to Voss's *Luise*; for it hardly seemed, with the dilemma presented in this way, that one could vote for both.

It was an aesthetic alternative; no moral issues were involved; for the one thing these two totally dissimilar poems had in common was perfect piety and the Lutheran creed. But Klopstock dealt directly with the cosmic mysteries, and never faltered in his manner of approach; too clearly inspired by his sense of awe to contemplate the anthropomorphic solution of the difficulty, so skilfully made use of by Dante and Milton to hold the minds of their readers enthralled. There seemed to be no other way out: either the eighteenth century must soar with Klopstock through illimitable space for what seemed like an eternity of time (there were nearly 20,000 lines distributed among twenty cantos); or it must sink to the level of the worthy pastor of Grünau, and sidle into his snug little house. It would be repaid for this lowering of the poetical flag by an abundance of luscious meals and picnics, flavoured by moral saws; but would not even the awful monotony of the blue empyrean be preferable to watching the snail-like progress of the course of a very dull love running very smooth? To be sublime with Klopstock or cosy with Voss; that was the searching question. To cease to breathe altogether in the rarefied atmosphere of Klopstockian altitudes; or to be smothered in a feather-bed of typically German *Gemütlichkeit*; to catch far-away strains of seraphic music in the *Messias*; or to take an intelligent interest in Luise's bridal finery. The experience offered by the one poet was too hard to undergo; and the experience offered by the other hardly seemed worth undergoing. Was there no other way out?

Goethe's *Hermann und Dorothea* showed that a little sorrow brought into Luise's existence would improve her vastly; and that Voss's cramped and complacent world could be given much greater emotional appeal if it were shown to be menaced, and this without departing by one tittle or jot from the indirect method of presentation. But this poem is exceptional in Goethe's work as a whole. Like all the great poets in the world, he was imbued with a sense of mystery ever striving to be expressed. His

19

evocation of the daimonic forces of nature in the *Erlkönig* has made him one of their spokesmen-in-chief; and no one has ever talked more hauntingly about predestined passion than he did in his murmured monologue to Charlotte von Stein about the transmigration of souls. Acutely aware of the essential mysteriousness of life as he was, direct expressions of it pervaded his works. Even when everything seemed to exclude the possibility of their intrusion, they somehow managed to penetrate. What in the name of commonsense were Mignon and the Harper doing among those sordid, squabbling and delightfully disreputable strolling players in the first draft of *Wilhelm Meister*? Adrift from the world of Ossian, they were also, alas, the harbingers of something far less poetical than they! If only Goethe had not allowed them to slip into a first-class theatrical yarn (fascinating but incongruous figures from a different land), we might never have had to cope with the portentous secret society which ruins the story at the end. In the same way, if Ottilie in *The Elective Affinities* had been kept within the bounds of the indirect method, we should probably not have been asked to accept the unpalatable mixture of magic, miracles and mysticism as a panacea for the social problem of marital and extra-marital love.

Theoretically (as I have already indicated) there

is everything to be said for the mingling of the direct and indirect methods. But it depends on how it is done. And I have sometimes wondered whether some of Goethe's longer works do not present such grave critical problems because he lacked the facility which Shakespeare possessed of modulating harmoniously from one key to the other. This naturally brings me to *Faust*. No two readers, I suppose, ever think quite alike about the problem of the Gretchen tragedy in the completed poem. In the *Urfaust* the web is woven with so cunning a hand that the mysterious warp cannot be disentangled from the ambiguous woof. From this point of view alone, the summit of poetical perfection was reached, and a supremely beautiful balance established. But not finally, and not for long. When the *Urfaust* was assimilated into *Faust Part I*, the two methods were struggling for pride of place. The cosmic nature of the conflict, emphasised in the prologue and the opening scenes, had to yield ground as the play went on, and revenged itself cruelly in the *Witches' Sabbath* by disrupting the organic course of Gretchen's tragic scenes. Aesthetically as well as ethically the whole scheme was obviously in the melting-pot, neither was any real fusion attained in the second part, in which mystery triumphed in the *Classical Witches' Sabbath*, held the stage in the *Helena* act, and had the last word in the mystical grand finale. Gretchen and Helena, each supremely beautiful in her own way, stand for Goethe's greatest achievements in the two modes; they are so far apart from each other that they cannot be compared; and the attempt to make Helen talk Gretchen's language (when she begins to speak in rhyme) is quite as incongruous as the plagiarism from the past which the ethereal penitent, 'once called Gretchen', utters at the end.

Symbolism masking obscurity is apt to increase in the works of poets as they grow old. Shakespeare, Goethe and Ibsen are cases in point. But Goethe was the scene of a battle-ground between the direct method of lyrical poetry and the indirect bent of creative genius. Looking at his work as a whole, one can hardly fail to see that his lyrical gift outlived his creative powers, leaving him to express his ever-deepening sense of the mystery of life sometimes lyrically, sometimes symbolically and more often philosophically as the years went by. This is his private history. The public part he was called upon to play was that of a portent for posterity. The depths upon depths of mystery concealed and revealed in *Faust* have ever since lured and beckoned to his compatriots. He gave poetical life and form to the fateful dynasty of questions which have haunted them through two centuries, and haunt them still. It is hardly too much to say that every

German poet since Goethe has dreamed (sometimes very idle dreams) of writing a *Faust* of his own. And by that I do not mean the hundred and one versions of the actual theme his countrymen have produced since 1808. The critics watch for Faustian productions, and hail them when they come: '*The Mirror Man* is Werfel's *Faust*; Kafka's is *The Castle*!' How often, and often how truly, such remarks are made. And even when this object is neither sought nor achieved, the desire to attain to equal profundity and to grapple with the same insoluble questions, has certainly accelerated the process of that growth in intensity in German Literature to which I have referred.

This, of course, would not have happened if there had not been a natural predisposition towards it; and the closer you look, the more clearly you discern love of obscurity lurking in the German poets. Schiller, in whom a dramatist was linked with a philosopher, began to yield to the direct method after grappling with the profundities of Kant and the insoluble mystery of fate. No one has ever yet been able to disentangle external destiny from internal fate in the course and character of his *Wallenstein*, which is of course as it should be, and is what gives to this unequal masterpiece something of Shakespeare's quality. But Schiller (unlike Lessing) failed to keep his head in the presence of one of the most alluring of the dark dynasty of questions; and *Die Braut von Messina*, in which the chorus carried the burden of the fateful message in touching imitation of the Greeks, is one of those resounding failures which could never have been perpetrated by a lesser genius; and that is perhaps to say, by a greater humorist. The same lack of aesthetic *savoir-faire*, although less glaringly displayed, is also evidenced by the dramatist Friedrich Hebbel, too apt to lever the mystery immanent or latent in his stirring dramatic actions into a transcendent position in the plays.

So great is the lure of mystery over the German mind that even such writers and works as appear most removed from it are generally drawn into its orbit. A signal instance of this is the naturalist Gerhart Hauptmann, whose masterpiece in the indirect method, *The Weavers*, one of the greatest works which the late nineteenth century has to show, was followed by a complete right-about-face into the opposite manner, a gyration which one can actually see taking place before one's eyes in the drama called *Hanneles Himmelfahrt*, the bridge between Hauptmann's naturalism, and *Die Versunkene Glocke*, Hauptmann's *Faust*. And in our own day have we not witnessed (and been rather sorry to see it) the creative path of *Buddenbrooks* forsaken by Thomas Mann for musings on the

Magic Mountain, whence he has descended like Moses, bearing tables of wisdom?

Yet we are probably wrong to repine against a tendency which we certainly cannot arrest. For the effort made in Germany in the nineteenth century to deal faithfully with the external world in novels of everyday life was not particularly successful, whether the indirect method was harnessed to straight realism, poetic realism or hard and fast naturalism. The Young German writers did their best, but never made anything tolerable of their problem novels and plays. Some later names certainly command respect. But one need only pronounce them: Gustav Freytag, Adalbert Stifter, Otto Ludwig, Gottfried Keller in the same breath with Balzac, Flaubert, Dickens, Thackeray, Turgenev and Tolstoy to underline their merely national prestige. Nor has the ambiguous muse of comedy often smiled upon German poets; and when she has done so, it has sometimes been a sardonic grin. So that, take it all in all, one must look outside Germany for the great triumphs of oblique art.

Germany, on the other hand, is the foremost exponent of the direct method, in which Goethe's *Faust* led the way for modern Europe. It might never have followed, however, or followed from much farther away, if the German Romantic Movement had not initiated those perilous voyages of discovery into the mysteries of nature, of the past, of the world, of the universe, and of the human soul. They led strangely enough to such unexpected results as the founding of schools of oriental philology, a positive spate of translations, and the psychological therapy of to-day. But these were only by-products. The rest of Europe pricked up its ears, England in particular. France at first turned the voyages of discovery into mere pleasure-cruises in search for local colour, or into sentimental journeys or gripping ghost-stories; but French poets too gradually became affected (perhaps I should say infected) by the prevalent nostalgia for the mysterious, the inexpressible, the unknowable, which caused a revolution in European letters whose final outcome cannot yet be foreseen.

It all went very deep in Germany itself. Never perhaps has the sense of the past combined with despair of the present and visions of the future resulted in anything comparable with Hölderlin's elegies and prophetic hymns. And a deeply romantic conception of life, and the tragic discord at its very heart, inspired that great poetic mythology of Schopenhauer's to which the generations after him succumbed. Nietzsche gave a direct answer to it in *Zarathustra*, speaking a language which belongs to the apocalyptic tradition, continued (at times in comminatory vein) in some of the later poems of Stefan George. Rilke projected a vision of radiant and dazzling angels against the dark background of a universe inexplicable and remote. These direct expressions of the riddle of life are towering crests on the waves of tragic lyricism racing over the ocean of mystery towards unseen horizons; a good and sufficient reason why those who are drawn into the study of modern German Literature persist in it until they drop or die. It is as if they were being helplessly lured onwards, perhaps to their doom, into the labyrinthine approaches of Kafka's *Castle*, which seems to retreat as they painfully advance.

Perhaps to their doom. Undertaken seriously, the quest is fraught with risks. The not inconsiderable hazard of losing one's sense of humour and proportion by the way has to be faced. Sooner or later one is almost certain to catch oneself out talking solemn nonsense in a mystifying jargon. It is a caricature of the modern German direct speech; which in itself is an intensification of a characteristic of the type as a whole. Milton could be rather emptily grandiloquent; Shelley occasionally soared into the inane; and Victor Hugo actually evolved an aesthetic theory to account for his frequent lapses into bathos when dealing directly with the sublime. This is the pitfall which besets the feet of those who endeavour to express the inexpressible by direct means. A definite loss may also be incurred in urbanity and civility. Civilised behaviour is apt to go by the board when fundamental issues are at stake. It is the ease with which the Germans have cast it off in some of their works that arouses apprehensions. In prose, especially, they insist too much; they become strident, as Nietzsche too often did; they go too far; they go too deep; they go on far too long. Some latter-day German critics of the direct type have sinned very gravely in this respect, doing violence to their subjects, becoming intolerably bombastic, and seeming to cooler minds than theirs to be mystery-mongering flagrantly. And altogether in the long run something rather intrusive about so much digging and delving becomes evident. The Sphinx of the Universe, one begins to feel, is entitled to a little privacy. This is a wholesome feeling, and one to be encouraged; it may save the student of German Literature from paying too high a price for his pleasures.

For the gravest result of surrendering oneself whole-heartedly to the lure and glamour proceeding from such transcendental works, is a sickness of the soul, a disease easier to diagnose than to cure. A divorce seems to have been effected without our knowledge or consent between our spell-bound minds and the simple, sober, permanently valid conditions of human existence. The intense preoccupation with realms outside our experience has unfitted us, if only temporarily, for the society of ordinary, everyday men and women. Must human beings be presented under direct cosmic rays in order to be seen poetically? Tradition answers no. Would Falstaff have fraternised with Faust? Or Mrs Gamp with Mignon? Would not even Don Quixote rebel against joining in the search for the blue flower of the romantic poets in the dark forests of the mind? And are they any the less poetical for that? For those with steady vision, are they indeed any the less mysterious?

It would hardly seem so to judge by the behaviour of the aesthetically uninitiated. The poetical probationer is perfectly capable of blundering into the *Iliad* and beginning to lecture Achilles on his lack of public spirit. He is more than ready to take sides hotly for or against Anna Karenina and Vronski. In this he undoubtedly resembles a country cousin addressing the wax-works at Madame Tussaud's, except that silence will not undeceive him. Perhaps nothing ever will. But trapped in the mazes of Shelley's *Prometheus Unbound*, he knows only too well that he has lost his bearings and is sorely in need of a guide. The one method conceals, the other reveals the mystery of the craft, and both have so much in their favour that it is impossible to choose between them aesthetically.

Historically, however, a discrimination can be made. Poetry, deriving as it did like all the other arts directly from religious ritual, must have been sealed with the mark of mystery at the beginning. What knowledge we have of old inscriptions, papyri, charms, spells and incantations, together with the story of the evolution of Greek drama, bears this out, and seems to suggest that indirect poetry came later and represented one of the victories of civilisation over the mysteries of blood-sacrifice and panic fear. One can at least say that, in becoming indirect, it took a long step forward towards disinterested and non-utilitarian art. This tends to become too 'pure' in the much abused sense unless quickened with its counterpart. Over-sophistication, artificiality, aridity and even down-right flatness are some of the forms of the Nemesis that lies in wait for indirect poetry carried to excess. They had created a desert in the literature of Germany by the beginning of the eighteenth century; they seemed to be menacing it again in the post-classical period. The reaction was correspond-ingly and increasingly strong. What began as a romantic hankering after a more primitive type of poetry, instilled into his countrymen by Herder (who is responsible for much), developed into a deeper and more dangerous passion for the dark, elemental aspects of life. Bachofen's *Matriarchy*

(1861) called a frenzied cult into being at the turn of the century; and the orgiastic attitude towards women displayed by some of the expressionist dramatists shows the same influence. These phenomena represent an exaggeration of something which probably always underlies the will-to-mystery. When that uncompromising spirit seeks aesthetic expression, it naturally makes use of the direct method.

The fact that this method is gaining ground in Europe is, I think, a symptom we should not disregard. As the chorus comes sweeping back into the drama, bringing mystery in its wake; and as we measure the distance between Joyce's *Ulysses* and Homer's *Odyssey*; between Pirandello and Sheridan; between Valéry and Villon, too; or as we compare and contrast (to quote from examination papers) Eliot with Browning or Balzac with Proust, certain conclusions must be drawn. Something is happening to poetry because it is happening to life. That is the merest truism. But (and this is a cause for misgivings) it seems to have originated in German poetry before it attacked all life. From the whirlpool of German Romanticism, waves of deep questionings and deeper pessimism about human values and happiness have been spreading outwards in ever-widening circles, engulfing mind after mind and country after country, too. To turn away from

31

a life, poetically speaking, no longer worth living to the great dynasty of questions beyond has been the natural result in literature, which became increasingly expressive as the nineteenth century waned and the twentieth century waxed of a half-divine, half-satanic discontent. It is the Faustian habit of mind, the pre-eminently German habit. It is far, indeed, from ignoble, and it probes very deep. But the spirit of this earth rejects it, you will remember, and it is finally obliged to consort with a demon who denies and tries to destroy everything humanity holds dear. It uses the direct method in poetry and achieves wonderful works of art. It uses the direct method in life and exterminates it on the grand scale. The best and the worst that Germany has to give to the world seem to be inextricably combined.